CW00821474

Also from Clevedon Community Press

Writing on the Lake:
an anthology of poetry and prose, 2016,
ISBN: 978-0-9935666-0-8

Thirty-three writers, drawing on vivid memories
and imaginations, celebrate the restored Marine Lake
in Clevedon through their poetry and prose.

CLEVEDON CUTTINGS

history, houses and a couple of characters

ABOUT THE AUTHOR

Jane Lilly was born in The Knoll Nursing Home many years ago and has never lived outside Clevedon. She has been researching the history of Clevedon since 1974 and probably will never find out everything she would like to know. She is not discouraged by this. The first of her many local history books was published in 1990, after she had already contributed essays on local topics to books published by Clevedon Civic Society Local History Group. Jane is now an Honorary Member of Clevedon Archaeological Society. She provided the information and images for the local history displays in the visitor centre on Clevedon Pier, Discover@The Pier. Jane is of the firm opinion that Clevedon is the best place in the known universe.

Clevedon Cuttings

history, houses and a couple of characters

Jane Lilly

Clevedon Community Press

Clevedon Cuttings

ISBN: 978-0-9935666-1-5

First published 2017 by
Clevedon Community Press
Unit 15, Tweed Road Estate
Clevedon BS21 6RR

Third printing 2021

Author: Jane Lilly
Cover design and illustrator: Stephanie Fitch
Copy editor: Guy Johnson
Printed and bound by: bookprintinguk

for everyone who has left me with happy memories – thank you

Acknowledgements

I am grateful to Clevedon Civic Society for permission to republish some articles from their newsletter. Many of these articles were published in the late Clevedon Mercury, and one in the Spotlight magazine, also out-of-print.

Help with illustrations has come as ever from Derek Lilly, David Long, Peggy Ruddy and Stephen Price as well as a private collector – many thanks to all of you.

And thank you to Angela Everitt, Co-ordinator of the Publishing Press Team of Clevedon Community Bookshop Co-operative, who acted as my editor.

Jane Lilly
October 2017

Contents

List of illustrations

Introduction

This book is a departure from my usual illustrated publications. A few years ago I wrote articles about subjects that interested me and gave them to local publications to use. I enjoyed writing and researching the articles and the readership never complained, thank goodness! My hope is that it was not my contribution that killed off the publications, as they have all become moribund since then.

The first three of these essays were written for my own satisfaction – New Clevedon: a Regency Paradise; Clevedon from 1830; Prospect House, Highdale Road. They have not been published before, although some material in the first two will be familiar from my introductions to previous books. The subject of the third essay, Prospect House in Highdale Road, was the home of my very good friend Stephen Price for some years, and we researched its history together with great interest.

Bristol House and Mount Elton both appeared in the *Clevedon Mercury*, having been written up as part of a larger research project of mine on our Regency town in which I hope to produce a history of each house built between 1790 and 1855. You don't have to be mad to do this, just take rather a long view!

The history of Oaklands, which stood in Elton Road until the early 1970s when modern flats and houses replaced it, was researched at the request of a Local History Group member – Sylvia, I hope you'll enjoy this! It has not been seen before.

The *Clevedon Mercury* was where the piece on Adanac House was printed, and the short item about Rossiter's appeared in a small magazine called *Spotlight*. It was triggered by someone asking me what our remaining oldest business was.

The rest are also from the *Clevedon Mercury*. For thirteen years I lived by Staddon's Barn in Parnell Road and was very fond of the building. The railway accident was too good to miss as I found articles about it in the *Bristol Mercury* to explain David Long's photograph. Doris Hatt was a dear friend of my late aunt, Marianne Youde, and the essay also appeared in the Civic Society newsletter.

Dr Noel Rudolf and I have been looking at the history of the old Hot and Cold Baths in Clevedon for some years now and, as I had a lot of material on the Marine Lake, I have combined the two subjects. It has been an enormous pleasure to see the Lake come to life again in the last few years as my father Bert Lilly was the first boy to join the local swimming club and swam there all year round. The last piece came partly from my researches for Clevedon Pier, where John Rowles was employed as pier master for many happy years, and partly from an interest in several families who moved here from the Framilode area of Gloucestershire in the 19th century.

I hope that a wider audience will be interested in these topics which I've enjoyed finding out more about – being nosey is a very satisfying pursuit!

Clevedon: a Regency paradise

Clevedon from the sea, c1860, anonymous print.

In 1799, the Enclosure Act for Clevedon was passed clarifying which of the waste ground and verges were commons. From here on the Elton family knew which areas of waste belonged to them as owners of the Manor of Clevedon. The commons were allocated to the various farmers leasing land in the Manor. The Manorial waste was a different matter, used in due course for the benefit of the people of Clevedon as well as for the Lord of the Manor.

Initially, the Clevedon Court Estate agent, William Hollyman, divided up verge land along the edges of what are now All Saints Lane and Walton Road and sold the plots to local people so that they could build dwellings for themselves. Houses in the cottage style followed and more plots were developed at that time in Old Street and Old Church Road, as well as in Court Lane, Tickenham Road, Kenn Road and Strode Road. All of these roads already existed, linking farmhouses to each other and linking

Clevedon to nearby villages. They followed the course of the rivers in the main, hugging the low land. The oldest roads in the village are all on the low-lying clay levels where surface water such as rivers and ponds could be accessed for domestic use.

The hills are formed of limestone, which does not retain surface water – this is why there were very few houses there early in the town's story. The only houses north of the low ground were Highdale Farm, where the steward lived from at least 1297 onwards, and Old Park House on Dial Hill: both of these houses had their own ponds as sources of water.

The Old Inn, c1900, anonymous print, author's collection, [the Hall and Woodhouse brewery wagon delivering in the foreground].

The first speculative development began at East Clevedon Triangle. William Hollyman built a row of elegant Regency houses in East Clevedon Triangle in 1821, Trellis Cottage with an attached shop and Ilex Cottage. The oldest public house, the Old Inn, stands nearby in the Walton Road, which forms part of the main route through Clevedon north and south. The photograph opposite shows this inn around 1900 when it still had the great bay window from which passengers for the coach could watch the road.

The first school was also in East Clevedon in a house that stood on the site of 2 Walton Road. It was run by a relative of the Elton family, Mrs White, who lived a life long enough to be teaching the grandchildren of her first pupils. She died in 1837 and her house was demolished and rebuilt in that year.

The main traffic passing through Clevedon in those days passed along Old Street where there was a smithy for the needs of the horses which were the main form of transport unless you walked. At The Triangle stood the Chipping Cross, formerly surrounded by the village green, where a weekly market had been held since 1346. The green was common land, enclosed in 1799, the first few houses appearing there in the 1820s and 1830s, followed by shops from the 1850s to the 1890s.

At The Triangle, travellers generally turned left into Kenn Road, the next part of the way through the town. Like most of the early roads, its name indicated its destination. It led southwards through the moorland villages and beyond to the Mendip Hills. Like the other two north–south orientated roads, Court Lane and Strode Road, it ran along ancient drainage dykes. Clevedon's low-lying farmland is known to have been drained by the 14th century.

With regard to road names, Clevedon has only one street, Old Street. Its old name was Old Village Street because it led to The Triangle, formerly the heart of the village and still called the Village by locals. Whereas a road is defined as leading from one place to another, a street has houses along its length. The main way through a settlement generally attracts some kind of income, witness the smithy, and there were farmhouses and cottages along Old Street in medieval times.

Returning to development, the next speculative building was put up by William Hollyman's older brother Thomas. He ran the Old Inn and was also a farmer, leasing land in the area of the The Beach. In 1823, he decided that he would extend his hospitality venture by building the Rock House, initially a tea house, low on the shore just north of the rocks where the pier was later erected. In 1824, George Cook was advertising four bathing machines on The Beach attended by experienced persons and drawn in and out of the water by winch.

This old print (anonymous) from a private collection shows the bathing machines on The Beach c1840, while in the distance on the extreme left, the low form of the Rock House can be seen in front of the taller building which is the old Hot and Cold Marine Baths.

The Beach, c1845, anonymous print.

This was a success despite being over a hilly mile from the Old Inn. British people had begun to travel far more in their own country during the Napoleonic Wars and, with the rise of the Romantic Movement, untamed countryside was a popular destination. A diary of a month's stay in Clevedon in 1824 describes the scenery and landscape in glowing terms, referring to the romantic situation of the Old Church, the glorious sunsets, shady woodlands and towering hills. Every aspect of the open air is mentioned, the perfume from hayricks, the sight and smell of wild flowers and the sound of the sea, as well as the birdsong.

The visitors keeping the diary were staying in Rose Cottage in The Triangle from where they ventured into the surrounding countryside and hills when the weather allowed, it being August. On several of their walks to the sea's edge, they visited the Rock House:

> Went down by a winding path to the foot of the rocks, where a neat house close to the sea is erected for public tea drinking. Went into the unfinished rooms, and returned up the rock home through the fields again.

In 1825, a young lady visiting Clevedon wrote to the Dorset poet, William Barnes:

> Cleavedon... just now becoming a resort for the gentry we went to the sea side near a mile from Cleavedon where we took dinner and tea at an Inn lately built in the rocks it is called the Shippaground it is the most romantic situation I ever beheld after we had taken tea we went on the water the gentlemen of our party each took an instrument of music so that we had quite a concert it so charmed the surrounding

villagers that in less than half an hour the rocks were covered with spectators.

By 1825, William Hollyman was well advanced in his own plans to benefit from Clevedon's projected expansion. The first house had been built on the Hill itself at 1 Highdale Road. William's ideas were on a larger scale and he bought a generous plot overlooking the sea to the north side of the old lane that led along the edge of the Old Park. The lane became Hill Road and he built the first hotel there, the Royal Hotel, in 1825.

Here were the beginnings of a genteel resort. In the next of my cuttings, the railway comes to Clevedon and the town begins to change more quickly and attract yet more visitors and businesses.

Clevedon from 1830

Clevedon from Dial Hill, c1845, anonymous print.

By 1830, those responsible for setting the level of rates payable in the town realised that they needed a survey to establish what new houses there were. This would form the basis of a new way of rating as the previous rates had been based on a list of farms. A great many new properties had been erected, with some still under construction, but the Survey (1830) lists twenty houses in East Clevedon Triangle and Walton Road, one complete and two incomplete in Highdale Road, eighteen complete and one being built in Hill Road, eight complete in The Beach and four more on the way to being finished, and work had begun on the first house in Wellington Terrace. The Hot and Cold Marine Baths were to be completed shortly where the vagaries of the tide could be outwitted.

The hotels at Clevedon, c1840, anonymous print, private collection.

The hotels are seen from the present Friary path: the Friary now occupies part of the Royal Hotel site while the York Hotel is in Marine Hill and was lately a convent.

More houses had been finished, built in the main by local people who saw a good chance of realising a return on their investment. Having finished one house, often the builder would raise a mortgage on that house to buy a second plot. One man, Thomas Poole, bought a wide plot in Hill Road on which he built five Regency houses and three cottages behind them on the steep slope. In the main, though, what happened was that, in the single house on a plot, the builder's wife would run the house as lodgings during the summer season while he continued in his trade. Sometimes she acted as resident housekeeper or, if her husband had been able to build a cottage or a smaller house on the plot as well, the family would move into that and let the entirety of their larger premises.

With the growth of the town came better road and sea links. The Bristol historian, Latimer, records an old Clevedonian as saying that in his youth, i.e. in the second half of the 18th century, as many as four wagons went from Clevedon to Bristol during a year. Other goods were carried by pack-horse. This soon changed as Clevedon grew, with the first coach service in 1824 leaving Bristol at eight in the morning and returning from Clevedon at six in the evening carrying six passengers. This cost 2 shillings per person – 10p. Ten years later there were three or four coach companies plying for trade on the Bristol-to-Clevedon route.

The sea route was easier, apart from the difficulties posed by the very high tidal range of the Bristol Channel which, without a pier, impeded the landing of passengers. In 1828, a pier was thought highly desirable and plans were solicited through the Bristol newspapers. In due course, one was selected and work began under the auspices of William Hollyman, working on behalf of the Reverend Sir Abraham Elton. It would seem that there had been a steam packet service to and from Clevedon in the 1830s because, in 1835, an advertisement for the Eagle steam packet states that

> in consequence of the danger and inconvenience upon landing at Clevedon, the packet will discontinue to sail for that place, until the completion of the proposed pier.

Sadly, the proposed pier was swept away in the storm in the November of 1837. It was another thirty years before a pier was again planned, successfully this time, by the Reverend Baronet's grandson, Sir Arthur Hallam Elton. However, the Pill pilots called at Clevedon to take visitors on sailing trips. Already there were donkeys for hire and a gentleman with an invalid chair could be hired to push those of poor health along the roads being laid out in what was being called New Clevedon. Sir Abraham Elton had by now seen the desirability of some open space for the public and he and his second wife, Lady Mary Elton, enclosed the old copse known as the Ripple which lay to the rear of The Beach. This formed what we know today as the Pier Copse and Alexandra Gardens, and gravel walks were laid out and benches set under the trees for visitors to use.

In the meantime, the first shops had been opened in Hill Road. Mr Edmund Gurney was a prominent grocer in the house behind what is now the shop Panache. He also ran a receiving-office for mail. The mails were dispatched from East Clevedon, from where a rider took them to Bristol. Among other early shops was the chemist's shop, now The Cellar, run in 1832 by Charles Stone. The oldest part of the shop is an exquisite survival having been built in the late 1820s on the plan of a quarter circle. The fitted drawers and counter follow that shape and are preserved within the current layout.

Drapers and dress shops followed and, of course, bakeries and shops selling meat, although the Eltons had wisely sold their plots with covenants on them limiting the trades to be carried on in premises built there to those free of noise and odour. This meant that the butcher had animals slaughtered at his other shop in the Village and sold the meat both there and in Copse Road. Copse Road was laid out in the late 1820s and the upper part developed during the 1830s. The part of that road backing onto The Beach is delightfully varied in character because houses were built on the gardens of the houses on The Beach only when the owners decided to sell off parts of their plots.

Most of the inland side of the Seavale end of Copse Road was built when the farmland became available, which only happened in the 1850s and 1870s at the end of the leases for those fields. Copse Lodge had been built c1835 and was a butcher's shop, but the two terraces date from the time when the fields were sold off for building.

The railway was a great catalyst in the growth of Clevedon after 1841. The main line from Bristol and Exeter brought a service as close as Yatton in that year, with the local hotel keepers providing light carriages at the station to bring guests to their accommodation. In 1847, a branch line from Yatton to Clevedon opened, seen here in a print issued to commemorate the occasion, bringing day trippers galore.

The railway line from the south, c1847,
anonymous print, private collection.

By this time, a great many lodging houses had opened too, as had an impressive number of small and select boarding schools. The railway often brought people into the town, from Devon and Wales especially, who either saw an opportunity to set up shop on their own account or sought employment. In the locality, going into service provided a welcome alternative to farm labour, and women, who had previously hardly been employed, were able to work at dressmaking or take in laundry.

The small boarding schools often catered for the children of those serving abroad in the tropics or in India who were eager to send their children to a healthy climate for an English education.

The trend lasted, in fact, until the closure of the well-known boarding school, St Brandon's at Clevedon Hall until the 1980s.

Prospect House, Highdale Road

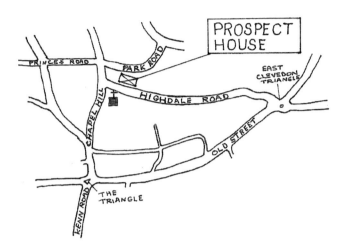

Prospect House was the first house to be built in Highdale Road on what seems to have been the first of the building plots sold by Clevedon Court Estate in that area. Elihu Durbin, a Clevedon tailor, bought the plot in 1824 and paid two years' ground rent of £1/8/6d in 1826, which indicates that the house was completed during 1825.

The new route from the sea to East Clevedon village was still under construction at this time and was eventually to become Hill Road and Highdale Road. In April 1827, William Vickerage supplied stone from Hangstone Quarry in Old Church Road for this project and laid eighty tons of small stones on the road which, by then, led from a cottage opposite the Old Inn to Mr Durbin's house at the western end of Highdale Road. The stone cost £4 (at a shilling a ton) and labour was charged at £5/18/2d. Numerous repairs were made in the following few years, as would be expected, as carriages and carts made their way along the new surface. The sides would become compacted by the wheels and the middle needed levelling or the carriage or cart body would 'ground' there. The path on which the new road was laid had, for centuries, been used for access to the Old Park on Dial Hill as well as to the large field system around Sixways, but needed much improvement as usage increased with the extensive building works undertaken in the 1820s and 1830s.

Prospect House, c2005, photograph Stephen Price.

In December 1827, James Panes was paid for assisting the surveyor Mr Townsend to measure out plots: 10/1d for six-and-a-half days' work. A gate kept farm stock from wandering freely among new houses being built as the land was still surrounded by fields. Joseph Cottle was often employed by the Estate to make new gates and made the one pictured and a few others in June 1827. On the next page, in a later print (anonymous), the gates can be seen across what is now Princes Road leading to the Hill Road and Highdale Road junction.

The wheatfields south of Hill Road, c1845,
anonymous print, Derek Lilly collection.

It is interesting to note that the new houses in various parts of the Hill were named to reflect the outstanding views that could be had from there. Though Prospect House was the first, Prospect Villa and Prospect Cottage, as well as Belvedere, all stood on the same corner of Hill Road and Highdale Road. Further along Hill Road, Bellevue, now numbers 41 and 43, stood facing along what is now Bellevue Road, named after the house. From this area, wonderful views to the east, south and west could be had, encompassing the Mendips and the Channel. In the Fir Woods, Bella Vista was built in the 1850s among carefully landscaped paths. This house was demolished about a hundred years later.

The bakery on the west side of Prospect House, Highdale Road,
anonymous drawing, private collection.

Returning to Prospect House, in 1830 John Luce bought the property which he leased in 1833 to Thomas Maynard a baker and confectioner. Maynard had recently inherited property from his father, a market gardener in Barton Hill in Bristol. He was investing in a new bakery business on his own behalf. In 1835, he was paying rates for Prospect House, a farm known as Childs & Mainstones in Old Church Road beside the present Library, and his newly built shop in Woodfield Cottage at the Hill Road end of Copse Road.

From 1837, Mr Luce let Prospect House to William Nichols, who seems to have expanded the premises with a shop, following which his rates went up by approximately 20%. In the drawing on the previous page, from a private collection, you can see the shop at the west side of the house with a fine large window. By 1842, William Nichols, later to become the town's much-respected postmaster, had moved to Old Street. Thomas Maynard was back at Prospect House and the property was now listed as 'house and bake-house'.

The next occupant was Mrs Harriet Laurie, who had been in business as a lodging house keeper at Trellis Cottage in East Clevedon Triangle since the death of her husband in 1826. She advertised lodgings at Prospect House in 1848 in *Hunt's Directory* and, in 1851, she had two lodgers staying at the house. Ten years later, one of them was still there, a mason called Nathaniel Perry, along with six other lodgers or visitors. Nathaniel married Ellen Newton, the landlady of the Rock House in 1863, but died the following year.

Mrs Laurie continued to rent Prospect House after it was purchased by William Cook, a Bristol rope and sail maker, with several other Clevedon properties in 1858. He was married to Amelia Balding in 1861 and, by that time, was clearing a site beside Greenfield House in Hill Road to build Goldwell, a large Gothic house unjustly known locally as 'The Ugly House'. He died in 1864 and his widow, Amelia Cook, continued to let Prospect House and the other properties. In 1863, Mr and Mrs John Stuckey were tenants at Prospect House. They were also lodging house keepers and the bakery side of the business seems to have lapsed. Two years later the house was empty but, in 1866, William Marks and his family moved in and were to stay until 1918 when the Great War ended.

In 1868, the Local Board of Health received a complaint from Mrs Laurie who had moved into the neighbouring villa at what is now 5 Highdale Road when she left Prospect House. She was concerned that a photographer's studio was being built on the premises at Prospect House. Presumably she was not happy about the siting of the building or the idea of the chemical smells which might emanate from it. Unfortunately for her, the Board felt that they had no jurisdiction in the matter and Henry Goodfellow, the photographer, continued his plans for a new small business on Mr Marks' premises. Mr Goodfellow advertised in 1868 offering a wide range of portraits and landscape photographs.

From the census returns and the burial records of St. Andrew's Church, a crowded house and some sad events would seem to be a way of life for the growing Marks family. In 1871, William, his wife Emily and their seven children shared the house with two visitors, ladies with independent incomes. These eleven people shared what originally had been a house with only four bedrooms, although the old shop extension provided a fifth bedroom. In *Kelly's Trade Directory* that year, William advertised himself as a confectioner, pastry cook and biscuit baker and was evidently a very capable man. In 1872, their oldest child, Emily, died aged nineteen, which must have been distressing for them all. The family lost another child, Florence, aged two, in 1875. They were still letting rooms to visitors and the grief and hard work had to be dealt with simultaneously.

In 1881, William had taken on a bakery assistant who lived with them; Emily had a general servant who also lived in. Together with a paying guest and their remaining six children, this again made a total of eleven people to be fitted in. By this time the older children were of an age to be working in the business. William Henry was working with his father as a cook confectioner, George was a baker and Rosetta assisted in the shop. The bakery was prospering and Mr Marks was soon able to better himself by buying the premises from Mrs Cook, his landlady, in 1878. It was at this point that he put forward plans for expansion to the Local Board of Health.

It was not until 1881 that the buildings were finally completed, but to the west he built refreshment rooms with accommodation above. These were later used for many years as grocery shops under various owners. To the east were his handsome new bakery buildings with two large walk-in ovens and rooms above.

The new refreshment rooms had a far larger footprint than the old shop and had two rooms above as opposed to one. This would have meant that the eleven occupants of the premises could have the use of six bedrooms in total, a far easier proposition with young adults and guests in the household.

In 1879, Marks was promoted in the local guide book with not only the usual 'cook, confectioner and bread baker' heading, but also

> soups, jellies, cream and ices to order, entrées of every description. Garden parties supplied. Wedding breakfasts and ball suppers by contract or otherwise. Plate and glass on hire.

The business continued to expand and provided the catering for events such as the harvest home feast in Kenn. The rooms were also used for pleasure parties, as advertised in the *Bristol Mercury* in June 1882, soon after their completion.

A case reported in the *Bristol Mercury* in 1888 shows Mr Marks as helpful to those in his trade – also that his fellow bakers were at times a slippery lot! Alexander Coombes fell into debt while trading in Old Street and borrowed some flour from Mr Marks. The intention seems to have been to allow Coombes to keep his business going and get out of debt while continuing in trade. In time, Coombes moved to Somerton after being forced to sell up and, in fact, inherited the sum of £225. This would have enabled him to pay off his remaining debts, but he was persuaded by his father-in-law, Mr Durman, that there was a way round this by claiming that his property all belonged to Durman. The judge seems to have been familiar with the wiles of Mr Durman's sort and Marks was paid back £12 including costs.

By 1891, William and Emily were entering their early sixties. Their daughters, Ada and Rosetta, and their son George, were still at home and involved in the day-to-day running of the bakery at Prospect House. William Henry had married and set up home in Queen's Road at 2 Osborne Villas with his wife and three small children.

In February 1894, Mrs Marks had applied to an agency in Bristol, who found her a house servant and charged 2/6d for the privilege. In September of the same year, she was surprised to answer the door to a young woman called Nora Cotter seeking a bakery job that didn't exist. It seems that the unfortunate Miss Cotter had paid the aforementioned agency 2/6d to find her work and had been given Mrs Marks' address. The agency failed then to write to Mrs Marks on her account. The poor girl paid her own train fare to Clevedon only to discover that she had been cheated – as it transpired, two other girls had also applied for the same non-existent post. Following this, the agency quietly shut up shop, with quite a few sums of money having been gained in this way from people who were out of work when there was no unemployment benefit to assist them. It was a rotten business all round.

It seems that William retired from running the business and signed it over to William Henry in 1900. William Henry seems to have had great ideas of expansion. By 1905, he had set up a restaurant at 11 The Beach, now trading as Tiffin, and continued to run it successfully alongside the business at Prospect House.

He advertised boldly:

> *W H Marks and Son, high-class cooks and confectioners,*
> *1 Hill Road and 11 The Beach, Clevedon.*
> *Continental confectioners and chocolatiers.*
> *Dejeuners, receptions, garden parties etc,*
> *of the most recherché description.*
> *Estimates and price list on application.*
> *Correspondence address: catering depot, 1 Hill Road, Clevedon.*

By this time, his brother Frederick had bought the chemist's shop at Marine House in Hill Road, now The Cellar, and set up his own long-running business, Marks the Chemist. The family continued as chemists here until the 1980s.

At Prospect House, however, the bakery came to an end in 1918 when William Henry retired at the age of 63, selling his properties here and on The Beach. He moved to Lower Weston near Bath.

The next owner was Thomas Henry Fry, farmer at Portbury House on the Kenn Road, who in 1921 let the premises to Mabel Rawlinson on a yearly tenancy. She had the shop, dining room, kitchen, yard, bakehouse, four bedrooms with offices (lavatories and washing facilities) and a garage in Park Hill. In the meantime, he sold the premises to a Mr Cryer, who died in 1922. Poor Mrs Rawlinson found that times were very hard and, in March 1922, she was forced to write to Mr Cryer's executors to say that, until the season started, she would be unable to pay her rent of £16/5/0d on the next quarter day. She would have paying guests over Easter and could pay at that time. She also gave notice that she would give up the business on September 29th that year.

In the lease, an inventory of shop fittings is given which throws some light on the way in which it was set out in those days. There was a two-light gas pendant in the window, gas bracket, three roller blinds to the large window, a brass curtain rail and two uprights, ebonized and gilt shelving on two walls, a pitch pine counter, a long arm for the outside blind (one small side window was cracked) and two desks in the small room adjoining. Outside there was a roller sun blind in good condition, a sign and iron rods. The emphasis on sun blinds stresses the fact that the shop faced south west, where the sun would shine in for much of the long summer days and would be blinding for those few winter customers.

The next purchaser of Prospect House was Mrs E A Jones, who shortly sold to Mr and Mrs R E Parsons, who, in turn, sold the place to a Mr J Dellow. In 1925, he took the step of redeveloping the bakery (east of the house) to form a small house, retaining the style of the shop to the west of the house. This house is now number three, Highdale Road, called Southview Cottage. The bakery is the present owner's sitting room and the old walk-in oven to the front of the house is now a dining room with a kitchen built into the equally large rear oven.

As for the shop adjoining the west side of Prospect House, Mr Dossett ran a grocery store there in the 1920s. Mrs Hannaford took on the business in 1930.

An interesting point raised by the study of this house is that, following Mr Durbin's five-year occupation after building was complete, it was not again owner-occupied until Mr Marks bought it in 1878. This fully illustrates the type of speculative building which went on in Regency Clevedon.

Bristol House, East Clevedon Triangle

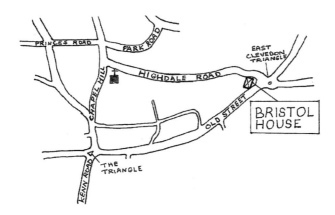

Bristol House today has the look of a house and shop never altered since it was built in a position commanding the East Clevedon Triangle. However, although this is in fact the case, there was an earlier Regency house on the site, Rose Cottage.

The involvement of the Long family in the development of this part of East Clevedon seems to be far-reaching. Richard and James Long had purchased land in East Clevedon Triangle and Walton Road and by 1798 they had built the first house on East Clevedon Triangle, number five, now adjoining Ilex House.

By 1831, it would seem that Richard had made enough money as a butcher to build more houses. The 1830 Survey records only a piece of ground on the Bristol House site. In 1832, his oldest daughter Ann was living in a house called Rose Cottage on the tongue of ground that projects into East Clevedon Triangle between Highdale Road and Old Street. She was twenty-eight and is very likely to have let rooms there. The house was south facing, rectangular in shape and projected at the east end into Highdale Road. This was eventually to prove its undoing.

Bristol House, c1990, photograph Derek Lilly.

Ann Long continued to live there until she married George Tilley, or Tilly, in 1833. He was a carpenter five years her junior and they had three children during their marriage, George, Edwin and Emma. By 1837, the rates show that the house belonged to the Eltons – perhaps the lease had finished or some agreement had been reached. At any rate, in October 1838, Rose Cottage was advertised for sale in the *Bristol Mercury*. The Tilleys moved across the road to live at 5 East Clevedon Triangle.

It was a shopkeeper, Henry Wood, who agreed to buy the land and Rose Cottage. The eastern half of the house was to be demolished to widen Highdale Road, which, by then, was one of the main access roads to New Clevedon with its genteel villas and lodging houses on Hill Road, Wellington Terrace and The Beach.

Rose Cottage shows on the 1839 Tithe Map and certainly would have constricted the road at that point. Given the steepness of Chapel Hill, and the fact that until Elton Road was laid out, Highdale Road was the best route to the Hill for carriages, the house had to go!

Henry Wood made the sensible decision to clear the site and start again. In fact, he built the present Bristol House, a square Regency style building facing west, with a small forecourt to allow customers a comfortable browsing area by the large shop windows. With the house he also purchased two orchards, one adjoining the rear of the shop and one which was part of what had been a larger orchard on the south side of East Clevedon Triangle.

The 1841 Census relates that Henry Wood was forty-two, two years older than his wife Anna. Their children were Henry aged eleven, Alfred aged nine, Amelia aged seven and Eliza Matilda aged two. Of these, only Alfred survived to adulthood. He became involved in the ownership of the property at the age of twenty-five in 1857, as above, with his father's executors. There was also a general servant living at the shop, John Brassett, aged fourteen. Two years after this, in 1843, Henry himself died and Anna ran the shop herself until her own death in 1851.

The business would seem to have been thriving, and worth burgling, as reported in the Bristol Mercury only two months after Anna was widowed:

> Charles and Joseph Davis and John Price were charged in suspicion of having been concerned in a burglary at the house of Mrs Henry Wood at Clevedon. It appeared that, Mrs Wood's shop having been broken open on the night of the 27th of February, and money and goods to a considerable amount stolen, a handbill was issued, describing three persons by whom the robbery was supposed to have been committed, and offering a reward of £10 for their

apprehension. P. S. 17 said the prisoners were apprehended that morning, in Charles-street, Bedminster, in consequence of their precisely answering to that description. They were ordered to be taken before a county justice. *[Bristol Mercury 1843, March 4]*

A few short months after Anna Wood's death in 1851, when the next census was taken, William Coombes Collings lived at Bristol House, a young man of thirty-two with his wife Sarah aged twenty-five. William's nephew was the thirteen-year-old errand boy who lived in, along with an assistant for the grocery and drapery, Elizabeth Barber, twenty, and the oldest staff member, Mary Clark, the thirty-one-year old general servant.

Ten years later, the family had grown considerably, with Arthur aged seven, Sarah aged five, Frances aged three and Margaret aged one living with their proud parents. There were three servants: Ann May, a draper, William Pollet, a grocer, and Eunice Goldstore, a general servant. They stayed for two more census returns.

In 1870, William Coombes Collings had already run and occupied the premises for almost twenty years having taken them over as tenant in 1851. In 1857, the owners were Charles Knowles, Alfred Wood (son of the previous owner), Charles and Thomas Taylor, Abiezer Harper and Jane Morgan (I think Henry Wood's executors), and Collings remained as their tenant after the house and shop were put up for auction. It would seem that Collings bought the premises, and the surviving rates show him as owner-occupier in 1869. A lease of 1870 from Somerset Heritage Centre records him as apparently entering into renewed ownership, holding the shop and orchards from the Eltons. It is this lease from which the details of the earlier house on the site emerged.

Bristol House, East Clevedon Triangle, c1925,
photograph, author's collection.

By 1871 Arthur Collings was nineteen and working with his father in the shop. The family additions since 1861 were William and Edith. Evidently the accommodation was a little stretched as the only live-in servant by this time was Martha Fowler from Clapton, aged eighteen.

Sarah, the Collings' oldest daughter, married John Hellier of Bristol in 1879 and settled in Bedminster so, in 1881, her little girl Elinor was staying in Clevedon at Bristol House. The oldest son Arthur is not listed and may have married and left home to set himself up in business elsewhere, but the four younger Collings are still at home, along with Walter Fisher a grocer, draper Annie Lockyer and the domestic servant Adelaide Portch.

William Collings retired and moved out of the shop in 1885, at which point Mr Hassell took over the business. By 1890,

Mr John Lloyd and his sister Alice from Radnorshire were running Bristol House with two draper's assistants and a house servant. It seems to be John Lloyd who acquired an extra shop in East Clevedon Triangle, the smaller premises adjoining Trellis House.

At some point a few years later, they sold both shops to Silas Dyer, who was to remain there for many years to come, having moved there in the late 1890s from his previous shop in Marine Parade. This postcard shows the shop when Mr Dyer owned it and ran it also as a Post Office.

Mount Elton, Highdale Road

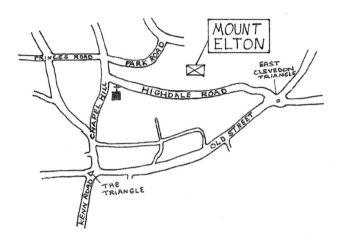

This house, designed by Samuel Whitfield Daukes for Lady Mary Elton, the widow of the Reverend Sir Abraham, is a beautiful example of the Elizabethan or Tudor style popular in the 1840s. It was completed in 1844, two years after Sir Abraham's death. Daukes also designed Witley Court in Gloucestershire and became a well-known and respected exponent of the Eclectic school of architecture.

The garden was laid out carefully by Her Ladyship, who had already with her late husband supervised the planting and layout of the Fir Woods north of Highdale Road. Together they had put a great effort into planning open spaces in Clevedon, setting out gravel walks and ordering the construction of stone seats in the old area of woodland known as The Ripple behind Copse Road. Under their supervision the woods formed the Pier Copse and Alexandra

Gardens. At first these were accessible by leaving a deposit for the key with Mr Gurney in Hill Road, but, in years to come, were gifted to the town by the Elton family as public open spaces.

Evidently Lady Mary realised what a quiet and pleasant south-facing area there was below the Fir Woods while she was working on them with her late husband. She was given two- and-a-half acres of land in March 1842 by the Elton family for her house of retirement, Mount Elton.

Mount Elton, print undated, private collection.

George Weare Braikenridge, an antiquarian and wealthy merchant from Brislington, was a great friend of Lady Mary. Together they had endowed and built Christ Church in 1838 and shared a common interest in ancient architecture and the re-use of what we now call 'architectural salvage'. His influence would seem to be demonstrated in the Great Hall at Clevedon Court where a feature known as the 'Wake' doorway is actually made up of two antique fireplaces believed to be from Bristol. As Margaret Elton says in her 'Annals of the Elton Family', Mary Elton was encouraged by Braikenridge to give the Great Hall an older appearance with the addition of the coats-of-arms of English monarchs painted around the window, stuffed and mounted stags' heads and chocolate brown paint.

Mount Elton has a number of features shared with both Claremont and Braikenridge's other Clevedon house in Hill Road, Newton House. The wood-panelled doors are linenfold, fireplaces are Tudor-arched, as are many of the door-openings and the main stairs have been designed with a heraldic bear holding a shield on the hexagonal newel post, harking back to the first Elizabethan age. The great 'grisaille' window lighting the first landing is leaded in the form of coats-of-arms and stretches almost from floor to ceiling.

A year after the completion of the house, Lady Elton lived there with her sister Jane Stewart and their niece Jane Euphemia Brown. These ladies inherited the house in their turn after Mary's death and were both devoted to its welfare. In 1859, the first Vicar of All Saints' Church moved into Stewart Cottage in the grounds of Mount Elton. He and Miss Brown married and occupied the house in their turn.

This Vicar was Stephen Saxby, a man of great intelligence and academic distinction. He was an authority of international status on astronomy and was made a Fellow of the Royal Society a few months before his death. His wife too was noted for her quick intelligence, an author of religious poetry, hymns and children's rhymes.

Mr Saxby died in 1886 aged only fifty-five, having been Vicar at All Saints for twenty-six years. Mrs Saxby spent much of her widowhood making sure that the house would be well cared for after her death, entrusting her nephew, Henry Noel Shore, a Commander in the Royal Navy and son of her sister Lady Teignmouth, with Mount Elton's future and writing often to him about its upkeep, as well as the rights that came with its ownership.

In 1888, she bought the land opposite the house to ensure the survival of her extensive views.

Mount Elton Footbridge in its heyday

On Mrs Saxby's death in 1898, Henry Shore inherited Mount Elton having been resident there with his aunt after he retired from the coastguard service in 1891 on grounds of ill health. It was he who proposed a rustic bridge spanning the road in 1896 to link the house to the land bought by Mrs Saxby on the opposite side. On the previous page is a pen & ink drawing of the once very pretty rustic bridge, a popular subject with the postcard manufacturers.

As George Case writes in his essay on the house in '*Clevedon from the village to the town*' (published by Clevedon Civic Society in 1981), there were objections to this idea from the local authority on three grounds: sheer novelty, possible blocking of the view and that the bridge was likely to frighten horses. The bridge eventually came into being in 1898, but coloured Commander Shore's view of the local Council, as one can tell by his statement about a later application for the building of a pony shed:

> it is proposed to construct this edifice of stone, brick, wood and possibly mortar, and it may in time be used as a loose box for a pony or other quadruped...

Clevedon Cuttings

Oaklands, Elton Road

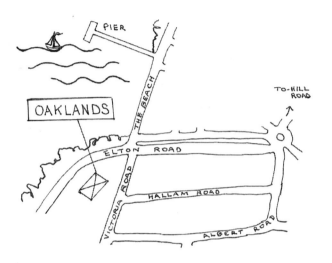

The story of Oaklands begins with William Andrews, a local carpenter who bought a large plot of land in Hill Road in 1828. On it he built Prospect Villa and Venetian House in partnership with George Biss. Biss then retained Venetian House, leaving Mr Andrews the remainder of the plot to the rear of both houses, bordered by a footpath which is now Park Road, leading to what was the Old Park.

Mr Andrews went some way towards developing this plot, building the houses now called Belvedere Cottage, Bycullah, Wayside Cottage and Highland Cottage, as well as Venetian Cottage on the higher ground behind Mr Biss' house. His son, William Henry Andrews, continued his father's work, calling himself Henry William Andrews to avoid any confusion. It was he who would, I believe, come to build Oaklands, in its day the largest house in Elton Road.

Building plots were first advertised for sale in the Bristol Mercury in September 1851 for what was to become Elton Road. George Somerton had already built the two pairs of imposing villas either side of what would become the junction of Elton Road and Victoria Road. The plots were generous, having a frontage to the road that varied between 90 feet and 255 feet. Buyers were to apply to Mr Thomas Ward, the agent for Clevedon Court Estate, for further particulars and a sight of the plan of the plots.

By 1853, Arthur Elton was deeply involved in building large private houses on behalf of his father, Sir Charles, for rental investment. Notably, he had begun to build in Little Harp Bay, where he would complete The Hawthorns, the Thatched House and Fairfield, all in Elton Road, which was then newly laid out. Of these, only the Thatched House survives – it is now The Little Harp public house. The other large house built at this time was Bella Vista, tucked away in the Fir Woods above Highdale Road and later renamed The Arches. That too has since been demolished leaving only its stables behind, subsequently converted into a private house.

In January 1853, Arthur Elton and Henry W Andrews were in discussion over a land purchase near The Hawthorns. It would seem that Andrews already had the adjoining plot and was eager to buy a little more to enlarge that plot – to which Arthur Elton happily agreed. By February the following year, Andrews had tentatively named the house Elton Villa and was giving Arthur Elton first refusal at a price of £2,000. It seems that this was refused and that Andrews felt free to put the house on the open market.

This was the house that became Oaklands.

Oaklands, c1930, postcard, David Long collection.

The first owner I can trace is Miss Metford, a lady who belonged to the Society of Friends. Miss Metford came from a family settled in Bristol and Long Ashton and was in her sixties when she moved from Failand House in Wraxall to Oaklands. She was very comfortably off, her family having been importing linen and occasionally wine into Bristol for some forty years.

She was eventually to lie in the Redcliffe Burial Pit in Bristol, the Quaker burial ground, along with her parents, Joseph and Hannah Metford. Her father was present when the foundation stone of the central part of Bristol Royal Infirmary was laid in 1788. He became one of their finest surgeons. A branch of the family in Long Ashton was involved in importing wine and linen and held part-ownership of several trading vessels.

The first glimpse of Harriot Nickleson Metford's arrival in Clevedon came when she moved to Oaklands in spring 1856, advertising furniture and effects for sale. Presumably these were surplus to requirements after she'd moved into the house and placed her possessions as she wanted them arranged in the rooms there.

At various times Miss Metford's nieces, the Misses Wright, lived with her and it is evident that she was well thought of within her family as three of her younger cousins and nieces were named after her. In 1861, the census lists those staying in the house with her, among them two nieces and two cousins. The servants were a lady's maid, a general servant, a cook, a butler and a manservant described as 'assistant in house'.

Miss Metford herself seems to have been a good mistress. After staying with her for twenty-seven-and-a-half years, one of her servants in Wraxall received an award at the Agricultural Show in 1855 for long service. She was generous to the poor and gave donations to the fund to aid distressed glass makers at Nailsea, as well as making several donations to the Orphans' Asylum founded in Bristol by George Muller. She was interested in her gardens and, in 1861, three bunches of her Muscat grapes grown at Oaklands won first prize at a floral fête in Bristol Zoological Gardens.

Sadly, in 1868, Miss Metford died and her properties were sold off. In addition to Oaklands, she still owned 21 Berkeley Square in Bristol where her father had lived, and a shop with rooms above at 36 Maryleport Street in the city. She also owned shares in the Clevedon Pier Company and Clevedon Water Works.

Here is the auction description for Oaklands giving details of the size of the house and grounds:

> A most capital and substantially-built freehold residence, with excellent Coach-house, Stables, Grapery, Conservatory, Storehouse, Lawn, Pleasure Ground and large productive Fruit and Vegetable Garden, containing together upwards of two acres, called Oaklands, situate in the best part of Clevedon, a rapidly rising and fashionable watering-place on the Bristol Channel.
>
> This charming residence is fitted up with every convenience, and has for several years past

been in the occupation of the late proprietor, Miss Metford.

It contains handsome entrance-hall, large double drawing room, dining-room, library, housekeeper's room, servants'-hall, china and butler's pantries, kitchen, scullery, dairy, larder, and other offices, nine bedrooms, two dressing-rooms, water-closets, store-room, etc.

The pleasure grounds are tastefully laid out, the graperies are planted with the choicest vines, and the gardens are stocked with fruit trees of the very best sorts. *[Bristol Mercury, 1868, 26 September]*

In the October of 1868, the house contents not wanted by the remaining members of the Metford family were likewise auctioned.

The 1871 Census reveals that William P Barrett, a gentleman of independent means from Bideford, was living in Oaklands having presumably purchased the house at auction in 1868. He was aged fifty-seven, twenty-six years older than his wife Mary. Their first six children, Alice, William, Robert, Frances, Walter and Algernon, had been born in Rodborough in Wiltshire and were aged from nine to one year old. The newest little Barrett, Douglas, was born in Clevedon and was six months old, so the Barretts had been in Clevedon under a year but more than six months, judging by the ages of those two youngest children. They kept house with a cook and four general servants.

At all events, in the next year they were on the move:

Somerset – for sale, a first-class freehold marine residence, with extensive Conservatories, Wall and Flower Gardens, Lawn, Stabling, Coach-house and

Yard, called Oaklands, situate in the picturesque and fashionable watering-place of Clevedon, on the Bristol and Exeter Railway, about eleven miles from the city of Bristol. This excellent residence is admirably built of Bath stone, and is not only in the most complete repair throughout, but has been improved and decorated by its present owner at a very considerable cost, and in the best possible taste, whilst every domestic arrangement is of the most perfect kind, and as an elegant house it has hardly an equal in the neighbourhood. The house, which is most salubriously situated in a genial climate, is nearly in the midst of its productive gardens and luxuriant shrubberies. The aspect is south-west and elevated, overlooking the Bristol Channel, and commanding extensive and delightful views of the Welsh hills and surrounding country. It is impossible to compress within the limits of an advertisement an adequate description of this elegant and much-admired property. Its beautiful and healthy position is too well-known to require comment, whilst its internal conveniences are of the most elaborate description, the whole being of modern construction and erected with the best and most durable materials, regardless of cost. It contains together nearly three acres. Price moderate. Gas fittings and fixtures at a valuation. To treat, apply to Mr Morris, Auctioneer, Surveyor and Estate Agent, North Curry, near Taunton; of whom cards may be obtained, to view. Dated Guyon-House, North Curry, near Taunton, May 20th, 1872. *[Bristol Mercury, 1872, 25 May]*

It is interesting to see the reference to Bath stone being used at Oaklands. H W Andrews also built Hampton House and Bassnett

House in Hill Road and fronted those houses with Bath stone too. All of these houses share a similar style of frontage and this makes me certain that he was the builder of Oaklands.

For the next five years, the owner of Oaklands was the Reverend John Lomax Gibbs, a nephew of William Gibbs of Tyntesfield in Wraxall. He had married Isabel Bright, a granddaughter of Richard Bright who had extensively researched the causes of kidney disease (Bright's Disease being named after him). They lived at Oaklands with their eight children. Before moving to Clevedon, the Reverend J L Gibbs had been the Vicar of Clifton Hampden in Oxfordshire until 1874. When he left Clevedon in 1878, he moved to Exwick where his uncle had greatly extended the church and parish of St Andrew there.

The house had changed somewhat in his time there, as you can see from the next sale notice:

Oaklands.

With conservatories, vineries, hot-houses, cucumber-house, potting-house, coach-house, loose-box, with coachman's rooms over; three-stall stable, with loft over; saddle-room, with man-servant's room over; fowl-house, [illegible], large stable-yard. Lawn and lawn tennis grounds, tastefully arranged pleasure gardens with large productive fruit and vegetable garden, stocked with the choicest trees, the whole containing 2 acres, 0 roods, 19 perches, (or thereabouts), facing the Green Beach, commanding most extensive and uninterrupted views of the Bristol Channel and the Welsh Hills, situate in the best part of Clevedon, a favourite and fashionable watering-place on the Bristol Channel, about 12 miles from Clifton, and now and for several years past in the occupation of the Rev. J L Gibbs, the owner thereof.

The residence, in the erection of which no expense was spared, is approached by a carriage drive and is replete with every convenience. It contains:-
On basement: good wine and beer cellars.
On ground floor: entrance hall, drawing-room, dining-room, morning-room, library, gentleman's cloak-room, housekeeper's room, servants' hall, china and butler's pantries, kitchen, scullery, dairy, larder and all necessary offices.
On first floor: seven bedrooms and a dressing room, three of the best rooms overlooking the sea; and three large rooms over.*[Bristol Mercury, 1878, 12 October]*

There was also a sale of surplus items and an insight into life at the house:

Plants of fernery, green and hot-houses,
Bay horse, 15 hands, good in saddle, also double or single harness;
A fat Berkshire sow, about 15 score;
Also, the grass keep of two fields up to the 25th day of March next, and one Mow of Hay to be fed on the ground; also, quantity of hay to be removed; a quantity of manure, garden wheelbarrow and roller, firewood, choice fowls, rhubarb, seakale, and other pots; lawn-mowing machine, glazed lights, pigeon-house and fan-tail pigeons, two targets and stands, hurdles, a large dog's kennel on wheels, small ditto, perambulator.
Also, furniture, consisting of a mahogany telescope table with oval ends and two insertions, several lots of carpets, some gas fittings, reading lamp, gilt cornice,

hanging wardrobe, nursery guard, linen press, foot bath, coffee mill and tin goods, three bird cages, a parrot's cage, pic-nic travelling tin, clothes horses, washing tubs etc. *[Bristol Mercury, 1878, 30 November]*

'Sale of surplus items ...'

In 1881, Joseph Nunneley lived in Oaklands with his wife and extended family. This included his mother-in-law and sister-in-law, as well as his son William, William's wife Georgina and their three small children. They employed a lady's maid, cook, house maid, nurse, butler and coachman. The rates for the same year reveal that the house was still owned by Reverend Gibbs, rateable at £102 a year.

The Nunneleys were of independent means, both father and son gaining their income from railway stocks and shares. It has been hard to discover more about them, excepting that sadly William died in 1884 at the early age of thirty-six. Since the late 1850s, the family had carried on a brewery business in Burton-on-Trent, and in fact only sold out in 1895.

In 1885, the local directory lists the house as still being occupied by the Nunneleys. This changed the following year when Mr Francis Berryman moved in having bought the house in May 1884. He was born in Wells, part of a family involved in the wool trade as well as importing wine and running a brewery. A relative of his, William Berryman, was a good friend of W F Lavington, also of Wells, who started a business in Hill Road selling wine and spirits in the 1850s.

The Berryman family had run a small brewery for some years in Wells in conjunction with their wine-importing business. Various members of the family were actively involved in the company until the firm merged with Bristol United Breweries in 1937.

Evidently the business had done exceptionally well for Francis, who retired here aged seventy. Oaklands was occupied by himself, his lodger Lucy Snelgrove, also from Wells and a lady of private means, and three servants, one of them a cook. The 1897 directory shows that Mr Berryman was still living in Oaklands at that time.

In 1901, the census shows that Ernest Wills was living in Oaklands having moved there from Frankfort Lodge, also in Elton Road. He was then aged thirty-one and was married to Maud, aged twenty-eight. They had two children, Dora, four, and Joyce, two. Maud's sixty-two-year old widowed mother, Caroline de Winton, also lived with them. Their staff consisted of a cook, twenty-four-year-old Jane Complin; Mary Parker, a nurse for the children, also twenty four; and a general servant aged twenty five.

Ernest was the manager of the Wills tobacco factory in Bristol. The Wills family retained Frankfort Lodge for a number years and Ernest's older brother, Sir Edward Wills, lived there after Ernest had left. Ernest and Maud had three more children while they were in Clevedon, Margaret in 1898, Barbara in 1902 and Ernest in 1904.

In 1911, the *Clevedon Mercury* directory shows Oaklands as empty and Ernest Wills living in Ramsbury Manor in Wiltshire with a large household in thirty-five rooms. Evidently he and his family and their entourage had outgrown even Oaklands despite his having added two bedrooms in 1908.

The house continued in the ownership of the Wills family and they seem to have used it as their summer home by the sea. When Clevedon was appointed as a convalescence base in August 1914, Ernest and Maud Wills offered Oaklands for use as a military hospital for the duration of the Great War. With the public spirit and generosity for which their wider family was so well known, they gave the house free of any charge.

Oaklands was run as a Red Cross Hospital, initially from the 2nd General Hospital in Bristol, being afterwards affiliated to the Beaufort Military Hospital in Fishponds, now known as Glenside.

The hospital opened in November 1914, after a great deal of hard work from the men's and women's VAD sections, from both Clevedon and Somerset. There were ten wards with a total of forty-five beds, as well as an operating theatre and dispensary. Over the course of the next few years, two huts provided twenty more beds, the tennis courts were made into an open-air ward and a billiard room, gymnasium and reading room were also contrived by converting outbuildings in the grounds. A large marquee provided still more beds to a total of one hundred and twenty. At this point, space was too short to allow of further development within the Oaklands estate so a house nearby called The Grange was rented on reduced terms from a local man and provided space for forty more beds and extra facilities.

In 1915, Lady Bellairs took over the neglected kitchen gardens at Oaklands, seen here in a contemporary postcard.

Oaklands garden, c1915, postcard, author's collection.

With a team of fifteen ladies she put them back into cultivation. The produce brought in some income to help run the hospital. This redoubtable lady also organised egg collections, the accounts and secretarial work. The full story of the Red Cross Hospital has been deeply researched by Rob Campbell, and I recommend his chapter in the Clevedon Civic Society book, *'Clevedon's own; the Great War 1914–1918'* as further reading.

At the end of the war, Oaklands was decommissioned and the house was offered for auction in 1919. The contents raised £900, which was put towards the building of cottage homes in Bay Road for disabled soldiers returning from the Front.

The house itself failed to reach its reserve. However, the *'Clevedon and District Directory 1923–4'* listed the Rev. D H C Bartlett and his wife in residence, and in the *'Clevedon and District Directory 1926-1927'* Mr Farrant owned it. In January that year, the *Clevedon Mercury* news roundup related that the Clevedon Urban District Council had been offered the house since they were seeking larger premises. The asking price was too high, however.

In March 1926, the *Clevedon Mercury* went on to report that a public referendum had been held as to whether Oaklands would make a suitable substitute for a pavilion and that the scheme had been turned down. The pavilion scheme had been one that groaned on for many years, with suggestions for such a variety of sites that one letter-writer put forward an idea via the *Mercury* that Clevedon should perhaps consider having a pavilion on wheels so that each site could take its turn!

At this point Mr Frank House stepped in and rescued the situation. He had a finger in several businesses in Clevedon relating to hospitality: the Creamery in Hill Road and The Towers Cafe in Marine Hill (recently a pub called Campbell's Landing). He purchased Oaklands in 1927 and made it into a hotel. In June 1928, the *Clevedon Mercury* proudly carried this large advertisement after Mr and Mrs House had made improvements:

Clevedon can boast the most ideally situated and best equipped Private Residential Hotels to be found at any seaside resort in the country in 'Oaklands'.

Standing on the sea front in its own charming and extensive ground of 3 acres, immediately on the Green Beach, a really wonderful panorama of the Channel and the Welsh coast is obtainable from most of its beautifully furnished rooms, and an unrivalled view of the glorious sunsets for which Clevedon is famous. When Mr and Mrs Frank House acquired the property in April, 1927, they spared no expense in completely modernising and reconstructing the premises, which were equipped in a manner equal to the best London Hotels, and it is worthy of note that the hotel has never been without visitors since the opening date, even through the winter months. The bookings for the ensuing summer season are very heavy. In fact, it was the increasing demand that made it imperative to extend the premises. Our photograph (not reproduced here) shows the new block of six bedrooms, with bathrooms and the usual accommodation, recently added to the Hotel. Plans for these extensions were prepared by Mr Inon J Leach (the Town Surveyor) and the building contract was entrusted to Messrs J Moore and Co of Nailsea, with the stipulation that the work should be completed by Whitsuntide. Not only was this stipulation fulfilled – the work was started and completed within six weeks – but Mr and Mrs Frank House inform us that the extensions have been carried out to their complete satisfaction. The new wing has been so cleverly planned and constructed in resemblance to the main building that it is by no means conspicuous, and no one but those previously acquainted with the premises would observe the addition. The whole work is a credit to Messrs J Moore and Co, and will enhance the good reputation which they have already established in this district for the way in which they carry out their contracts.

The new rooms have certainly a beautiful outlook. Three of them look direct out to sea, and the other three face the tennis court and gardens at the rear of the hotel. Like the other bedrooms in the hotel, they are all fitted with hot and cold water supply, Electric and gas lighting, with a head switch over each bed, electric and gas heating, electric bells etc, and electric plugs are also fitted in every room for the purpose of electric cleaning. The Hotel now contains 22 bedrooms, fourteen of which (together with two excellently equipped bathrooms) are situated on one floor. There is also a special ventilating shaft in each bedroom.

The furnishing of each room is a revelation to all who visit the Hotel, which will compare more than favourably with any similar establishment in the provinces.

Mr and Mrs House continued to own and run the hotel until 1936, after which Eustace Perry purchased the building. The latest listing I have is from *Kelly's Directory* in 1939 showing Mr Perry's continued ownership.

On the next page is one of a series of postcards of the hotel, showing the side view.

Oaklands from the side, c1930, postcard, author's collection.

John Bigwood pointed out to me that there is an excellent aerial photograph on the Britain From Above website (britainfromabove.org.uk) showing Oaklands in September 1949 as St Brandon's Junior School. As time went on, it became clear that the building would need a great deal of expensive renovation to continue in use as a school. The remedy was to sell the entire site for redevelopment, after which St Brandon's was able to build a new junior school in their own grounds in 1971.

Oaklands was demolished and new flats and houses were built on the site. These were put up for sale in the early 1970s and, for the time being, there the story rests.

Adanac House, Kenn Road

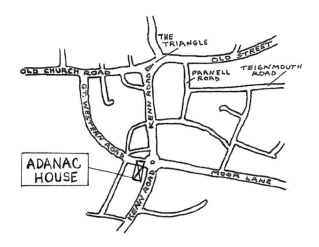

Poor old Adanac House was one of the casualties at the time when the motorway came to Clevedon. It stood where Great Western Road meets Kenn Road and was demolished to clear the route for Great Western Road along with a pair of houses in Oldville Avenue.

The name was given to the house by one of the occupants, Mr G 'Sid' Ware, a local man who had been to Canada, changed his mind and returned. The name is Canada spelled backwards. The house was built by Arthur Hallam Elton who, in 1853, decided that a lodging house was needed for single men coming to Clevedon for the building trade. His family had owned Clevedon manor since 1709 and had been at first absentee landlords. The family had begun to develop what was a small village as a seaside resort for genteel visitors in the early 1820s and the opportunity was now on the horizon to begin building on what had been farmland. Arthur

Elton took great care over the project, employing Mr Bindon of Pope and Bindon in Bristol as architect. Some twelve months after he first thought of building the lodging house, he was choosing the beds and bedsteads at Mr Candy's shop in Old Street, as well as discussing a suitable housekeeper.

Adanac House, the Employment Exchange, photograph undated.

That there was a need for so many extra building workers in the town was largely due to Arthur Hallam Elton himself. On behalf of his father, Sir Charles, he was undertaking a great many building projects in the town. They ranged in size from generous mansions to simple estate cottages. During the 1850s, he was to oversee the building of estate cottages in Old Church Road, Walton Road, Tickenham Road, Old Park Road, Strode Road, All Saints' Lane, Kenn Road and Chapel Hill. He also built Public Hall at Sixways as well as large private houses such as The Hawthorns, Fairfield, the Thatched House and Bella Vista (soon afterwards renamed The Arches). He had the National School in Old Street rebuilt in larger form to a plan by Pope and Bindon in 1858.

So there was certainly a need for extra lodgings for working men – the plentiful holiday accommodation available in Clevedon was needed for visitors to the town. The lodging house plan shows that downstairs the intention was to have three bedrooms, a large communal living room, a kitchen, scullery, tool room, wash room with three basins, closet, lobby and modest sitting room. Upstairs was laid out as a dormitory with eleven cubicles. I take it that there were privies outside. Sheds and a pig sty were planned on the half acre plot.

When the building projects finished, the house became redundant and, in Mr Chapman's 1868 *Guide to Clevedon and Neighbourhood*, we read that:

> ... in the Kenn Road you will see a building of gothic character opposite the termination of the Moor Lane. This was originally built by Sir Arthur Elton as a lodging house for single men, but being found only partially successful, it has since been let to two benevolent ladies, resident in Clevedon, who have established a school there for girls, either orphans or neglected by their parents.

These two ladies were Elizabeth Jacob and her widowed sister Mary Russell. They were two of the daughters of William Jacob, a Fellow of the Royal Society, expert on the international corn trade and former MP. He amassed a large fortune trading in South America and, as his son predeceased him, his daughters would have been considerable heiresses. Of his three daughters, Mary and Lucy married, but Elizabeth lived with him until his death in 1851. In 1859, Elizabeth Jacob was staying at Woodspring House in Hill Road, while they purchased The Grove in Walton Road. In 1860, the directory lists her and Mary Russell as residents at The Grove. It seems that they lost no time in setting up the orphan school, as it was listed in the 1861 Census.

The sisters were very comfortably off and evidently both had a social conscience. The servant school, as it is listed in the census, accommodated the matron, an assistant matron and eighteen girls as boarders aged from ten to sixteen. Eleven of the girls were from Bristol, the rest from other places in England. Ten years later, in 1871, there are twenty-four girls there aged from ten to eighteen, with a matron, under matron and laundress.

One of these girls was Janet Lowe, who was born in 1855 in Manchester. She married in 1872 and had twelve children, as well as raising some grandchildren after one of her daughters died young. She lived until 1941, remembered well by her great-grandson, whose daughter, Sue Foster, gave me these details of her life.

Elizabeth Jacob was still paying the rates for the school in 1881, by which time she was aged eighty-one. There were, at that time, eighteen girls there aged from eight to fifteen. From a family researcher enquiring about the house a few years back I learned that two of them, Mary and Lucy Harrup, sailed from Liverpool to Quebec in May 1883 aboard 'SS Sardinian' under the 'Home Children' scheme. Their father had died, their disappeared and their younger brothers were in the workhouse in Bath.

Schools bringing up young orphans and abandoned children to enter a life of service abroad and in this country were widespread by this time. It is sobering to think how many children passed through the school at Clevedon – especially as they had very mixed fortunes after leaving.

The last listing I can find for it as a school for orphans is in the directory of October 5th 1889. The following week, the address is listed as occupied by Mr and Mrs Carter and called plain '33–5 Kenn Road'. By 1890, Mr and Mrs Childe were living there. Mr Childe was a schoolteacher and it may be that the couple ran a school there.

The next people living at the house were the Thomas family, who were coal merchants and ran their business from the house for several years. (Other members of the family traded coal at West End). Following this, the Parish Room for St John's Parish was there for a number of years until 'Sid' Ware came back to Clevedon from Canada and gave it the name that it's been known by ever since. He lived in the house and Mr and Mrs Holley ran the Labour Office there in 1937, a local directory tells us.

The late Ken Ball and his family were the final occupants of Adanac House until the new road layout meant that it was to be demolished. Great Western Road was laid out and opened in 1986. The Ball family still have fond memories of their old home.

Clevedon Cuttings

Rossiter's, Hill Road

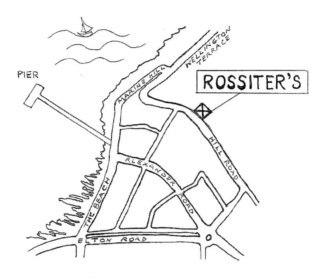

In the 1960s and 1970s, aside from going to my grandfather's old grocery shop in Kenn Road to buy the majority of our food, we shopped at Parker's Bakery, Seeley's stationers, Hagley's drapery shop, Ganniclifft's newsagent and occasionally Neale Brothers, although only occasionally at Neale's because grandpa sold ironmongery. His was the kind of grocer's business that smelled of cheese, fireworks, potatoes and leather bootlaces.

With the very recent closures of Seeley's, Neale's and Challicom's, I had a hard time thinking of a family-run shop of any age. Then I lit on Rossiter's the jeweller's in Hill Road.

Rossiter's, c1890, private collection.

The business was founded in Weston-super-Mare in 1832, but they appear in Clevedon in the 1871 Census when John Rossiter's son Ebenezer had lately set up a branch in the current premises in Hill Road, with his older sister Elizabeth as assistant. When a younger sister, Eunice, married Clevedon watchmaker James Perrett in 1878, they took over the Hill Road shop. When James died in 1915, Eunice continued in ownership until her death in 1934. Like the rest of the family, she had trained with her father in the Weston shop, and would have been perfectly capable of managing the shop and workforce.

Early in the 1900s, Rossiter's took over the business run by Mr Ralls at Greenwich House at 22 Old Church Road. Mr Ralls had made the works of the Triangle clock in 1898 and Rossiter's repaired the works in 1909. The Hill Road shop was under the name 'E Rossiter', and Greenwich House became 'J Rossiter and Sons'.

Now in the sixth generation of the family, Rossiter's continues with the Hill Road branch as well as the old shop in Weston and branches in Bridgwater and Barnstaple.

This advertisement is one of the earliest to feature the shop, published in an Almanac of 1871.

Rossiter's advertisement in the
Clevedon Almanac, 1871, author's collection.

Clevedon Cuttings

Staddon's Barn, Parnell Road

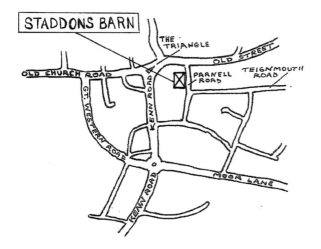

It is always a great pity when a community loses an old building, but I was especially sorry when Staddon's barn was demolished very recently. It stood in Parnell Road, formerly known as the Old Barton, or barnyard, and the old name reflects the age of the building.

Staddon's was a very successful business. They offered fencing, window frames, skirting board, floorings, doors, gates, rustic poles, hardboards, blockboards, insulation boards, formica and arborite in 1969, for instance.

Staddon's Barn, 2010, photograph Jane Lilly.

I have often wondered where the farmhouse stood that the barn belonged to, and Derek and I struck lucky a few years back when we found some Old Street house deeds that held the answer. The farmhouse itself is the rear half of 18 Old Street on the right-hand corner of Limekiln Lane and Old Street. At some point in the 19th century a shop was built between the farmhouse itself and the road. The shop and house have since been converted into flats and the first-floor flat to the rear, in the old farmhouse itself, has had its roof raised in the past to form a two-storey dwelling. The roof trusses from the earlier roof are still in place about a foot below the present ceiling.

The earliest beginnings of the farm lie with Thomas Barber, a Clevedon yeoman who left it to Thomas Churchouse to lease in 1742. It passed to Richard Owen of Nailsea in 1771, who, in turn, left it to his wife Hannah. The Barber family had an interest in it until it was sold to Thomas Hollyman in 1799. In all the transactions, a barn, stable and outhouses are mentioned, so the barn was over 250 years old.

The Parnell Road area was referred to in the old deeds as a 'mow barton'. This defined a yard with a barn where crops were stored. The barn stood at right angles to the prevailing wind and had high, wide doors. When flailing and winnowing took place, these doors were opened to allow the wind to blow the chaff away, leaving the heavier grain behind.

Thomas Hollyman's son John began to develop the land in the 1830s and much of that area of Old Street stands on the land formerly belonging to Barber's farm. Because the farm was freehold, the Elton family had no say in what was built so, although one or two houses of reasonable quality and size were built, quite a lot of very small cottages were squeezed onto small plots.

Limekiln Lane was in fact built entirely within the farmyard and several buildings between that and the old National school were also on land from the farm. Hollyman sold the orchard that lay south of Old Street from the corner of Parnell Road towards the Triangle to the Cottle brothers. The Cottles split the orchard between them and in total built a row of three houses now forming the carpet shop, cafe and pet supplies outlet, as well as half a dozen cottages and Moat House, a large shop with accommodation over, which was completely rebuilt as Woolworth's in the late 1950s.

In 1854, eleven acres of land with the barn and two cottages were bought by Ferdinand Beeston, a timber merchant who had rebuilt Salt House in the 1830s. He sold the property in 1858, at which time the barn was used by Edmund Candy, the grocer who had a large business in what is now the carpet shop. In the course of time, ownership came to John Griffin, listed as owner of the Barton and nine houses there in the 1876 rates. He married Brunetta Parnell, and Parnell and Griffin Roads were named after the couple.

In 1928, the rate book reveals that the barn belonged to Jack Brewer, who occupied the carpet shop I mentioned earlier as the Corn Stores from around 1910 into the years of World War II. The barn must have provided good storage space for him, particularly during the Great War when he was noted for gathering materials that could be salvaged. With the money he got for the materials he provided an ambulance for the Red Cross Hospital for wounded soldiers at Oaklands in Elton Road.

Roy Girling's excellent history of Staddon's in '*Clevedon's Social and Industrial Heritage*', published by the Local History Group, relates that Staddon's was set up by William Staddon in the station yard in 1920. He hasn't given a date for their move to Parnell Road, but says that they took over the barn from, 'a company building coaches, ambulances and similar vehicles'. I assume that company had the barn after Jack Brewer ceased to need it, and before Staddon's took it over.

Now the history of the site continues with its development for low-rise accommodation. Staddon's as a business has remained in Clevedon on another site.

The Railway Accident

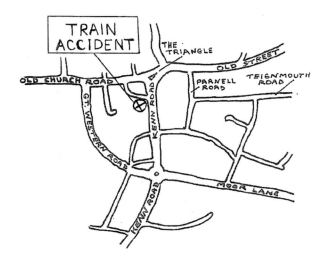

Oh, whoops!

As David Long's photograph on the next page shows, there were some pretty drastic slips between cup and lip for the careless train driver in the old days of the Great Western Railway in Clevedon.

This photograph was taken after an accident in April 1881, when the 6.28am goods train from Yatton, drawing eight coaches and three trucks, over-ran the platform. It hit a stationary train which had two coaches attached to its engine and drove them right through stop blocks and out of the end of the station, which had at that time a wooden wall.

The circumstances were, in many ways, fortunate given what had happened. Often passengers arriving in good time were wont to take their seats in the train, but no-one was on board. Because it was so early in the morning, very few people were up and about in the road itself, although a milkman had a lucky escape being only a few yards away from the station.

Railway accident, 1881, photograph, David Long collection

On landing in the road beyond the end of the station, the engine of the passenger train became embedded in the soft ground and came to a halt, but it was considerably damaged and the coaches were shattered. The driver 'whistled loudly for the breaks' *(sic)* said the Bristol Mercury reporter. This startled nearby inhabitants, although it would seem from the report of an earlier incident that it was routine when applying the 'breaks'. The crash following must have made a considerable noise and we must feel for poor Mrs Hack living opposite the station who was looking out of her window and saw the train rush through the station wall towards her house. It must have been the most frightening thing she ever saw!

Mrs Hack sees the 6.28am goods train come crashing through the
Clevedon station wall and onward toward her house!

The driver was described as one of the most steady men on
the line – in spite of which the directors at Paddington had
interviewed him and fined him £5 in addition to stopping his
annual bonus worth £10. Only his previous good character saved
him from dismissal.

The Bristol Mercury goes on to explain that crowds of
people visited the scene during the day, and that photographs were
taken before the wreckage was removed – hence David's good
fortune in finding this photograph.

A break-down gang came with an Inspector from Bristol,
Mr Burt, and removed the debris by drawing the engine back into

the station using two very powerful engines brought from Bristol for the purpose. Amazingly, the railway schedule was not disrupted at all, but the postal telegraph wire was broken, though soon repaired.

A train had emerged from the station into The Triangle before, in 1850, carrying a great many passengers coming to Clevedon for the annual ball. However, no-one was hurt even though the train hurtled through the wooden station wall into the road. The engine-driver and stoker escaped injury by jumping off. Again, the driver had blown the whistle to indicate that the brakes had been applied, but neglected to apply them. It seems to have been a dangerous contest between drivers to make the best time to Clevedon from Yatton, resulting in disaster for the wooden wall of the old station!

By 1898, the end of the station had long been embanked and stone-built. However, when the brakes truly failed on the 11pm train from Bristol, the stop block was wrecked and several timbers between it and the end wall of the station were damaged. The engine stayed on the rails, damage being caused in the main to the front part of it when it hit the stop blocks. The second coach was damaged when the first rebounded from its impact with the engine and the two coaches were lifted in the air as a result. Windows were smashed and cushions disarranged (what a dreadful thought).

This last comment in the 1898 report tickles me when the writer is explaining that this was the third time a train had over-shot the platform:

> A curious circumstance in connection with that event was the fact that a window was driven bodily out into the street without having one of its panes broken, and what is more remarkable is that years before when a somewhat similar accident occurred, precisely the same thing happened to this window.

Again, there were no casualties and the officials, after attending to the passengers, soon set to work to clear the line. They had to work far into the night to remove the wrecked coaches. The driver in this case, William Radford, was a very reliable character, one of the GWR's most experienced staff. Before he came to the Clevedon branch he had been the driver of the Flying Dutchman, and had never had brakes fail before.

Several more extracts from the Bristol Mercury, though not on the subject of the photograph at the opening of this cutting, cast light on some curious happenings. In 1856, a set of false teeth was found near the station and advertised for collection. If not claimed within three weeks, they were to be sold – not a pleasant thought these days.

Mr Armand D'Oursy, a professor of language teaching at the Reverend Stephen Cornish's renowned private school, Walton Lodge, had the misfortune to suffer a nasty fall when he thought to visit the gentlemen's convenience at the station before boarding the train. It seems that he managed to have disregarded warnings from the stationmaster that the convenience was out of use due to building work and that, if he used it, it was at his own risk. Lights had been removed, scaffolding erected and access was via a nine-inch-wide plank.

The professor persisted and, on this occasion, fell into a hole in the building, breaking several ribs and spending eight weeks in plaster. He had, it seemed, gone sixty feet beyond the entrance to the lavatory in the dark, struck a match and was seen to enter a doorway saying, 'Why didn't you put a light here, or tell me?' It was decided that, because he had a ticket, he was entitled to use the facilities, which ought not to have been closed to the public. He was awarded £24/10/6d damages, so it cost the railway a lot of money considering that all the professor wanted to do was to spend a penny.

Clevedon Cuttings

Doris Hatt

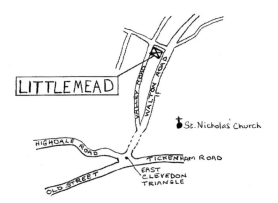

Older people in East Clevedon will remember the artist Doris Hatt and her companion Margery Mack Smith. Doris was a Christian Communist who sold the communist newspaper in the Old Inn and gave parties at Christmas for the local children. She and Margery were lifetime companions.

Doris moved to Clevedon in about 1922 having trained at the Royal College of Art and travelled in France, working with Ferdinand Leger, who had a great influence on her. She was born in Bath in 1890 and died in 1969 in Clevedon.

The house in Valley Road, Littlemead, was built in 1938 replacing the wooden chalet which Doris had inhabited until then. The architect was N H N Darby of Weston-super-Mare, who had built Sunway on Dial Hill Road in 1934. The two houses comprise Clevedon's sole Art Deco domestic architecture. In this drawing, you can see Littlemead from the side.

Littlemead

The interior was open plan and simple with a kitchen for Doris and another for Margery. Doris' studio could be curtained off from the large living space while Margery worked at the loom in her annexe added a few years after the main house was built.

I was lucky enough to meet Doreen Cooke, who was also a friend of the artist. Doreen has over a dozen of Miss Hatt's oils, watercolours and prints so, when the chance arose, we arranged a meeting at my house with Denys Wilcox, who photographed the pictures we had. Denys is researching Doris Hatt and her life with a view to publishing a book on her when possible. Fortunately I had recently been in touch with Andy Littlejones, who brought along two more paintings and a lot of ephemera kept by his uncle Mr Dyer, who knew Doris as a personal friend.

Doris Hatt with Sir Arthur Elton, c1960, private collection.

Having assembled a sizeable sample of 'Hatts' in one place, we found the range of colours and styles startling! In addition to her preferred palette of greens and reds, Doris also experimented with blue and greys, magenta and oranges and pinks and pastels. Much of the subject matter was local, but there were also West Country places featured. Still lifes were often depicted against a window as she loved to look out on the world.

Clevedon Cuttings

Sea Bathing in Clevedon and the Evolution of the Marine Lake

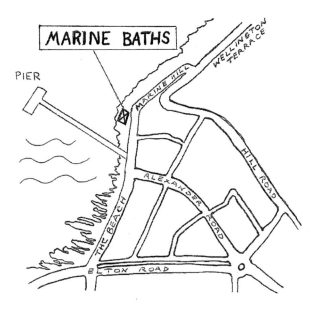

The first reference to sea bathing at Clevedon comes from the Bristol Mirror, when in 1823:

> George Cook respectfully informs the ladies & Gentlemen of Bristol and the public generally that during the ensuing season he will have Four bathing Machines on Clevedon Beach which will be drawn in & out of the water by Capstans. Experienced persons will attend the machines and every possible care will be taken.

Bathing machines were changing huts on wheels which could be drawn into the sea while the bather stripped and donned a long smock. When the door of the machine was level with the surface of the water, an awning could be lowered to give the bather privacy while descending the steps at the door.

Bathing machines in Clevedon

In 1828, Samuel Taylor of Hutton bought a plot of land now on the site occupied by a bungalow called Sea Walls, north of the Royal Pier Hotel. The level part of the plot provided enough space for Taylor to build a house, while the sloping cliff was low enough to allow the making of an enclosure which could be filled by the tide and would then retain seawater for the bathers. The importance of this on the Bristol Channel, where the range between high and low tide is some forty-seven feet at its extreme, was paramount if you were aiming to make your money from those who were bathing in sea water.

These Baths were still in full use when they were bought by Sir Arthur Elton in 1864 and thoroughly renovated. The bathing machines were still there too, run by the Lilly family, who rented the foreshore from Clevedon Court from the late 1830s.

By 1881, the proprietor of the Baths had to combine the business with a steam laundry to make the Baths financially viable. By 1883, the public rooms there were in use as auction premises. Enlargement of the existing site was impossible as it was surrounded by other properties, the road and the cliffs.

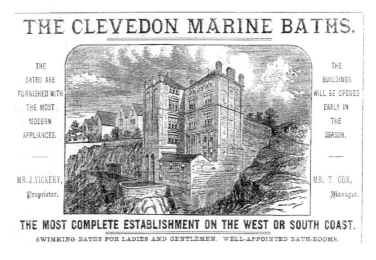

Baths advertisement in the Clevedon Almanac, 1877, author's collection.

This print depicts the much-improved baths seen from the pier. The print was used from the 1870s onwards in several guide books and almanacs on Clevedon.

The Clevedon Local Board of Health had discussed methods of making sea bathing and the Baths more attractive and viable from the 1860s, when the enclosure of Harp Bay had been suggested, along with later ideas such as the laying of a concrete base on the shore and clearing the mud to a point below the Salt House wall. In 1887, further schemes were put forward and none carried out. By the 1890s, the Board was involved in purchasing the Pier – the Baths plans, as well as a scheme to enclose Salt House Bay, fell by the wayside. By 1900, the Baths were disused and, within a few years, collapsed into the sea.

In 1907, the Council had bought the field called West Leaze from Clevedon Hall. They renamed it Salt House Fields and, in 1923, decided to develop it for recreation, providing unemployed men with work during the economic depression. Tennis courts were laid out, a wooden shelter built and plans agreed for the laying out of a footpath round Old Church Hill and Wain's Hill to form Poets' Walk.

In October 1926, Councillor Frederick Nutting urged the Council to enclose Salt House Bay. It was suggested that boating and bathing there could earn the Council as much as £200 a year, when the sea was only deep enough for bathing for approximately two-and-a-half hours a day. Clevedon's bathing income was entirely dependent on the tide table and brought in £155 a year.

Of the money for the Clevedon lake scheme, 75% would be spent on unskilled labour. 50% of the material was on site, and the Council had a bona fide offer of £240 for boating rights alone. The population of Bristol was three hundred thousand, and Clevedon was the closest seaside town with a decent beach and road and rail links. The enhanced income from bathing and boating would certainly pay off the loan for building.

A local enquiry was held by the Ministry of Health in 1927 and Mr E H Shopland supported the scheme, little having been done in the town to increase visitor numbers for some thirty years. An offer had now been received of £400 for the boating rights alone on the proposed lake. The scheme went forward and Mr Nutting purchased Salt House and sold the Council the woods behind the house at cost, improving access to Poets' Walk. The Crown sold the rights to the foreshore to the town for £150, and Mr Gower Pimm, the engineer, applied to the Mercantile Board of Trade for approval to build the lake.

In September 1927, tenders were put out specifying that 90% of the men employed must be local. This would ease the appalling unemployment situation in the town. The tender from Messrs J Moore and Co of Nailsea, at £5195/0/6d, was accepted. Work began after March 1928 on a slightly reduced plan which was to enclose an area of three-and-a-half acres.

The Marine Lake, c 1980,
photograph Joe Ruddy, Peggy Ruddy collection.

After decades of delays, the lake was in use in August 1928, generating income of a total of £62/11/3d in the first week alone. Clevedon Publicity Association had been granted the management of the boating and deckchair hire. The Council decided that they would run the swimming themselves for the first year.

At last, on March 30th 1929, the opening of both the lake and recreation grounds on Salt House Fields was performed by the

Lord Mayor of Bristol, Councillor W H Eyles. In his speech thanking the Lord Mayor for attending, Sir Ambrose Elton in fact said that Clevedon was offering

> a happy paradise for the toil-worn men and women, and especially the children, of the Lord Mayor's great and wonderful city, so that here they may enjoy themselves and recuperate their health. We hope that more and more of them will make use of the opportunities we are trying to provide for them.

This photograph shows the Lake when the entirety of the amenities were in place: from left to right, beyond the tree a small bandstand which later became the office, deckchairs for hire, the changing pavilion, a diving board, a teak slide paid for by the swimming club and a diving stage.

The Marine Lake, c1930, postcard, author's collection.

Captain John Gower Rowles, Pier Master 1893–1921

1897 Jubilee celebration at the pier,
postcard, David Long collection, [Captain Rowles second from left].

The three Rowles brothers, Elijah, John and William, were born in Gloucestershire in small villages near the junction of two major canals. Although their father and grandfather had been shoemakers, the boys in this generation of the family all took to the sea and worked along the Severn and its estuary, largely delivering coal up and down the Bristol Channel.

They worked together and, in 1871, the Census shows them as being aboard the trow 'Success', a collier of thirty-eight tons, registered in the Port of Gloucester and moored at Bridgwater when that census was taken. 'Success' was owned by G Sims from Saul, a village at the junction of the Thames and Stroudwater Canal with the Gloucester and Sharpness Canal. The latter canal was the deepest in the county, built to bring ships from the Severn to the Port of Gloucester.

William was the first to come to Clevedon, where he married Emily Hancock in 1875. Her father was a coal merchant and for a few years William worked for him until he could set up on his own. He later also leased Clevedon Pill, where he broke up old wooden vessels and sold the wood for re-use or for firewood. My grandfather, Thomas H Lilly, bought wood to make a shed behind his grocery shop in Kenn Road – he put a piece of wood from an old boat carved with the legend 'licensed to seat 37 able seamen' over the door.

At any rate, William and John both became master mariners and between them owned and operated several trows, including 'The Brothers', 'William and Martha' and 'Nellie' as well as the ketch 'Emily'. 'The Brothers' had been bought by them from Daniel Gower of Cardiff, after whom John was named.

John moved to Clevedon during the late 1880s. The Bristol Mercury reported in March 1888 that he piloted and berthed the first steamer to be landed at Clevedon Pill, the 'Dalrudda', commanded by Captain M C Keegan. The 150-foot-long vessel was carrying the first load of twenty-five thousand sleepers needed for the new light railway line between Weston-super-Mare and Portishead. The newspaper also said that it was a sign that the idea floated some years before, of constructing a harbour under the south side of Wain's Hill, was certainly possible.

In 1893, he successfully applied for the post of pier master on the newly refurbished pier. His salary was at first £60 a year and was increased to £80 the following year. Among his duties was the inspection of the local pleasure boats.

A sad accident occurred off the pier in 1895 when, for the first time in thirty-five years, there was a drowning near the pier. A small keel boat called 'Hare' had capsized in a sudden squall and one of the three men on board, all of whom were from Pill, north of Bristol, swam for the shore. His companions clung to the hull, but sadly one of them drowned before another boat rescued the remaining men. Captain Rowles lowered the pier boat and, with the help of his assistant Alfred Feltham, dragged for the body. which was soon recovered. The unfortunate man who was drowned had never been in a boat before.

On a happier note, the end of that year saw the pier celebrating the end of the steamer season. The 'Ravenswood', one of P and A Campbell's pleasure steamers, set off from Hotwells in Bristol on the last trip of the year, and passengers were able to enjoy seeing Clevedon pier brilliantly illuminated for the occasion, lined with people holding Roman candles and lights. The ship lingered while passengers and the folk on the shore sang 'Auld Lang Syne' before carrying on towards the lightship in the Channel to say her farewells there.

In 1896, the local boatmen asked John Rowles to revive the Clevedon regatta which had been in abeyance for some ten years after the previous organisers had moved elsewhere. He formed an influential committee and had the luck of dry weather on the appointed day, though the sea was rather choppy and the wind cold. The planned course was from one side of the bay to the other, with the pier hard being the best vantage point. One way and another, the start was delayed for so long that some races were held over to another day. Both sailing and rowing races proved popular, with much rivalry between Clevedon and Weston-super-Mare.

The Clevedon Promenade Band played on the pier head during the afternoon and evening and the regatta concluded with a procession of illuminated boats, a very pretty sight, as well as a display of fireworks. Clevedon lost the sailing race, but won the rowing. The Clevedon boatmen then raced each other, finishing off with an amusing sea-horse race at about eight in the evening.

In 1898, John Rowles proved to be a great friend to James Sims, an employee on the pier, when Sims' house was burned down. He instigated a collection to help the family who were uninsured and left more or less destitute. James Sims was from

Framilode where the Thames and Stroudwater Canal met the sea –
he was likely to be from the same family as Mr G Sims who had
sold the trow 'Success' to the Rowles.

In a wonderful memoir of the Bristol Channel's coasting
trade in which he spent his working life, Edmund Eglinton had this
to say of one of the Rowles' boats 'Nellie':

> She was owned and skippered by Captain W Rowles
> of Clevedon. In the last quarter of the 19th century
> Captain Rowles and his brother John owned two deck
> trows, the William and Martha and the Brothers. My
> father had sailed with them in both vessels and he and
> Captain Rowles were friends.
>
> The Rowles had a motorboat at Clevedon used
> for fishing in the winter and pleasure trips in the
> summer. This was very useful for, should the wind
> come in from the north west whilst the Nellie was
> discharging the boat could be sent down to help her
> get clear of the breakers from which the trow when
> light had to depend on her stern anchors and then
> kedges to warp her clear of the surf before sail could
> be set to try to claw her off the lee shore. If the wind
> proved to be too northerly she could be helped back
> into the river Yeo and there lie secure waiting for a
> slant to get her clear of the shore.

Fortunately, Edmund Eglinton's book, *'The last of the
sailing coasters'*, includes a photograph of Captain John Rowles, as
this helped me to identify him on this photograph loaned by David
Long. It is a postcard showing the pier approach dressed for the
1897 Jubilee celebrations and Captain Rowles, a tall, bearded man,
is standing in the centre underneath the star. He was aged around
fifty and living in the toll house with his wife Sarah and their niece,

also named Sarah, who helped in the house. The star and other illuminations were gaslit.

Captain Rowles was the pier master until 1921. He died in the December of that year in Framilode, having served Clevedon Pier for twenty-eight years.

Clevedon Cuttings

Further reading

Campbell, R. (ed) (2009) *Clevedon; medieval manor to Victorian resort*, Matador/Clevedon Civic Society.
Campbell, R. (ed) (2010) *Clevedon; places and faces*, Matador/Clevedon Civic Society.
Clevedon: the village to the town (1981) Clevedon Civic Society.
The Annals of Clevedon (1988) Clevedon Civic Society.
Clevedon past (1993) Clevedon Civic Society.
Clevedon's social and industrial heritage (2000) Clevedon Civic Society.
Clevedon; clubs, cakes, quarries and cash (2002) Clevedon Civic Society.
Clevedon's own; the Great War, 1914–1918 (2004) Clevedon Civic Society.
Clevedon at war 1939–1945 (2006) Clevedon Civic Society.
Lilly, J. (1990) *Clevedon in old photographs,* Alan Sutton.
Lilly, J. (1994) *Clevedon in old picture postcards*, European Library.
Lilly, J. (1999) *The Shops of the Old Village*, Clevedon History Series volume 1, Meaker's Bookshop.
Lilly, J. (2002) *The Shops on the Hill*, Clevedon History Series volume II, Darren Meaker in conjunction with Village Pump.
Lilly, J. (no date) *Fishley-Holland Pottery, Clevedon, Somerset*, North Somerset Museum Service.
Lilly, J. (ed) (2004) *Clevedon; Francis Frith's photographic memories*, The Francis Frith Photographic Collection.
Lilly, Jane S. with Lilly, Derek B. (2007) *Images of England: Clevedon*, Tempus.

Clevedon Civic Society has an excellent website at www.clevedon-civic-society.org

See also the local section at Clevedon Public Library, where there are out-of-print items.

Clevedon Cuttings

www.clevedoncommunitybookshop.coop